And then I Started Feeling Pretty...

Uproot the Lies, Replant the Truth,
and Live Your Life in Full Bloom!

Alicia Redmond

And Then I Started Feeling Pretty
Uproot the Lies, Replant the Truth,
and Live Your Life in Full Bloom!

Copyright 2019 © Alicia Redmond. All rights reserved. No part of this book may be copied or reprinted for commercial gain or profit. The use of short quotations or occasional page copying for personal or group study is permitted and encouraged. Permission will be granted upon request.

ISBN: 978-0-578-45694-2
2nd Edition

Author's Contact Information
AliciaRedmondMinistries.com

Published by:
Bloom House Books

"Books by women, for women."

Bloom House Books is a division of Fi Nix Six Media, LLC.

Scripture References
All scripture references are from the Complete Jewish Bible (CJB) except where noted.

Thank You

My Heavenly Father—Without You, I am nothing. Thank you for creating me just the way I am and choosing me for this work. I live for You and I love You.

Jocelyn Hairston—My friend for what seems like a lifetime… You have been in my corner as a sister, prayer partner, cheerleader, and coach! Thank you for the gift of you and your unwavering support.

John A. Calhoun—Thank you for being my accountability partner in the final push to complete this book! You are a true friend with a beautiful heart.

Layla—My sweet pooch! God, I thank you for bringing this faithful, little chocolate-colored joy into my life. I marvel at her happiness and unconditional love for me.
(Book coming soon ☺)

Dedication

To my Mom and Dad—You two are my greatest examples of love, resiliency, wisdom, kindness, strength, growth, even entrepreneurship and creativity, and most of all... forgiveness. I love you and I thank God for you always!

To YOU—The woman reading this book. I celebrate your wisdom, desire, and determination to be the woman that God created you to be!

Table of Contents

Reflection 11

Introduction 13

Chapter 1—The Seeds That Shape Us 21

Chapter 2—Walking Wilted 35

Chapter 3—The Master Gardener and You 45

Chapter 4—Uprooting 51

Chapter 5—Replanting 77

Chapter 6—W.E.E.D.S. 99

Chapter 7—Your Greatest Beauty 109

Conclusion—In Full Bloom 121

Journal Your Testimony 127

Reflection

When you look in the mirror, do you like what you see?
Is it a reflection of someone you don't want to be?
Someone too skinny, seems like you're getting fatter…
too light, too dark, too old to even matter?

When you look in the mirror what do you hear?
"You're so stupid!" "You're ugly… why bother?"
"Who's going to want you?" "Don't you wish you were another?"

All of these lies the enemy speaks, if you listen at all, you become weak— weak in spirit, weak in soul, weak in your mind, losing control.

But God has not given you a spirit of fear, but of power, love, and a sound mind—IT'S HERE!

On behalf of the Father, I SPEAK FREEDOM RIGHT NOW from the chains that have bound you—the enemy must bow— to the mighty name of

And Then I Started Feeling Pretty

JESUS! BE FREE in your soul—He came for the captive and those under control—of the adversary and all that is dark— you are GOD'S, you are healed, you are free, you've been marked—To receive His love and all that He is— all that He's done and All that He gives!

Joy and peace are yours for the taking!
Forgiveness and love– He's molding and making—you into the image of His beloved Son

He calls you to Himself
You are His
You are One!

And our loving Father says this to you…
"One with Me— One with man
Loving My people because now— you can!

Love Me with all your heart and love your neighbor AS yourself —This is the "true riches"— this is the "true wealth".

Being free to love is the best you can be—by this, they will know you—

That you ARE love—
A true reflection of Me!"

Introduction

Jeremiah 1:10 There! I have put my words in your mouth. Today I have placed you over nations and kingdoms to uproot and to tear down, to destroy and to demolish, to build and to plant.

We can all feel beautiful one day and absolutely hate our reflection the next.

However, if your feelings about yourself and your life tend to be more negative than positive, you're in the right place!

If you are ready to overcome the negative mindsets and internal blocks that have kept you stagnant, this book is for you.

If you desire to learn more about your identity in God, this book is for you.

And finally, if you want to learn how to love and accept yourself, just the way you are, this book is definitely for you!

So, get ready to embark upon a journey. A journey of discovery, healing, restoration, and most of all, a journey to LOVE!

A DREAM

As you read this book, you will notice that God speaks to me through the realm of dreams quite often. It is a beautiful gift, a part of my identity, and something I am happy to be able to share.

Several years ago, I had a dream that I lived in a huge mansion. Oddly enough, I only occupied a corner of the mansion; a small room that contained everything I needed.

On the other side of the door to my room was a hallway. That hallway had a door to the right that led to the rest of the house.

Around that door, a glimmer of light spilled into the cracks around the door frame. Life seemed to be happening on the other side of the door! I could hear people laughing and enjoying themselves, but I dared not venture outside of the comfort of my little room.

And Then I Started Feeling Pretty

Large windows with blinds surrounded the room. The space reminded me of a studio apartment, equipped with a kitchen, living room, bedroom, and of course a bathroom… everything I needed.

I stood in the bedroom area and caught a glance of myself in the dresser mirror. I drew closer. I had on a long fuchsia nightgown and robe (which I own in real life), my hair, also fuchsia, was in its natural state, twisted in an up-do, and my makeup was beautifully done!

I examined myself closely, (you know how we do) externally and internally. I decided I liked what I saw, and I smiled at myself. I liked who I was and who I was becoming… I felt "pretty". I realized that I loved myself, which was a revelation for me.

Suddenly, there was a crowd of diverse people at my window looking into my room. In a rush to close the blinds, I noticed that the people weren't looking at me… they were looking at my television. In dreams, a television generally means revelation, or something being revealed.

Upon waking, I knew the feeling I had in the dream was actually reflective of how I finally felt about myself in real life! I had grown to love myself... completely... as I am!

God not only affirmed the evolution of my identity in this dream, but He also addressed my fear of being "seen". He revealed to me that my purpose and calling wasn't "about me". It was about the "revelation", or message, He had given me for His people.

I want to give you the interpretation of the dream in the form of a prophetic word for you. If you are able, please speak it aloud. *(Faith comes by hearing...)*

Many of you have been in a "confined" place. Some have been confined by wounds of the soul and some have been confined through a series of events that have led you to this place. Even so, here, in this place is where you will begin to learn to love yourself. You will begin to gain an understanding of who you are and what you are called to do. You will no longer look in the mirror and dislike what you see. No, you will learn that what God has created by creating you, He calls "good"! He calls lovely! He calls perfect in every way!

You will come out of the place of confinement... the place of hiding, and you will be the light that you have been called to be! You will share of yourself, you will share your gifts and talents, and you will become the child of God, created in His image and likeness that you were called to be from before the foundation of the world.

You will not live in fear of stepping out, but you will live in faith! For the JUST SHALL LIVE BY FAITH! You will walk with the boldness of Christ and in full assurance and confidence in God that He is with you always... for He said in His Word that He will never leave you, nor forsake you. You will fulfill your assignment on this earth, and nothing shall be impossible for you because you believe!

Receive the word... In Jesus' name!

WHAT YOU NEED FOR THE JOURNEY

In my opinion, the following scripture is one of the most poignant when it comes to self-examination...

Proverbs 23:7
For as he (a man) thinks in his heart, so is he.

How you think about yourself matters!

What you think about yourself matters!

Your perception of yourself affects every area of your life; your identity, your calling, your relationships, and your purpose.

Prepare to take your time. This is something you will need if you want to receive the most out of this book. As you explore each chapter, there are several places for you to "confess" and share your truths. You will need to allot time to pray, think, and meditate. You can think of this book as a personal diary between you and God.

Therefore, keep a pen or pencil handy, and a journal or notebook if you are reading by e-book so you can write.

The Bible encourages us in James 5:16 to confess our trespasses to one another, and to pray for one another so that we may be healed. This is a part of our journey together.

My prayer is that this book will help facilitate healing for your heart, that it will give you a new perspective of your "true" identity, and that it will inspire you to live life abundantly as the woman God created you to be!

On the next page, I'd like you to record your initial thoughts, hopes, desires, or expectations about your journey.

And Then I Started Feeling Pretty

Chapter 1

The Seeds That Shape Us

1 Peter 1:23 You have been born again not from some seed that will decay, but from one that cannot decay, through the living Word of God that lasts forever.

"God says you're everyone's cheerleader! You will support others wholeheartedly, but you look in the mirror and think to yourself *you* can't do it. The enemy tried to steal your identity when you were around three years old, but God says He's going to deal with this matter quickly."

These were the piercing, yet truthful, words spoken by a prophet after a service I attended. He saw the deepest wound of my soul.

You see, my birth mother, Linda, was "taken from me" at two and a half years old. *(I will explain in chapter 3 why I use this phrase.)*

During a time when my mother and father were separated, she became involved with another man. My grandfather, her father, greatly disapproved of him. In his words, the man was "bad news"... and he was right.

She informed my grandfather that she planned to "break up" with him. A few days later she went to the man's house to tell him their relationship was over. He got angry, strangled her, then called the police to report his crime.

This was the seed that shaped me.

Although my father remarried a few years later, to my Mom, Janell, whom I love dearly, I wasn't aware of the trauma I carried in my soul from losing Linda. To be honest, none of us were.

We never talked about her... ever. There weren't even any pictures of her in our home. From my perspective, for the most part, we carried on as though she never existed. However, the trauma I carried was very real. As much as she was "buried" in my external existence, she was also buried deep within my soul.

As a child, between the ages of around 8 to 10, I had a recurring dream of losing my Mom, Janell, in a grocery store. I felt frantic on the inside searching the aisles for her, but I remained calm-looking on the outside.

Upon reaching the back of the store, to my right, I saw her eye-glasses laying on a tree stump, and to my left, I saw headless bodies thrown in a pile. Instantly, I knew her body was in the pile. *(There was no blood in the dream, so it wasn't as harrowing of a sight as it could have been.)*

There are many places in the bible that liken people to trees. For example, Psalm 1:3 — He shall be like a tree planted by the rivers of water.

A tree stump generally symbolizes someone that has been "cut down". You can refer to King Nebuchadnezzar's dream about the tree in Daniel 4:13-15.

Also, a headless body symbolizes that life, ideas, legacy, or what someone symbolizes has been "cut off" or destroyed, and there is no hope of the person ever coming back. Refer to the story of David and Goliath in 1 Samuel 17:51.

Of course, I had no idea what the dream meant as a child and I never shared it with my parents, but I now understand that it was a manifestation of the trauma of losing Linda, and the fear of losing Janell.

I also believe the dream was recurring not only because it was how I felt inside, but also because God wanted me to share it with my parents to help make them aware that I needed counseling. I often kept my feelings inside as child, hence, in the dream, being frantic on the inside, but remaining calm on the outside.

WOUNDS OF THE SOUL

Wounds of the soul can be inflicted several ways with many acquired during childhood.

Being rejected, abandoned, neglected, betrayed, abused, molested, experiencing the death of a loved one, and other traumatic events can leave you with unresolved hurt, bitterness, anger, resentment, unforgiveness, and other negative feelings.

If you don't acknowledge, address, and receive healing for your wounds, sooner or later, they will negatively affect your life.

GETTING TO "THE ROOT"

When you receive Christ, confessing Him as Lord and believing in your heart that God raised Him from the dead *(Romans 10:9)*, your spirit is made new, however your soul *(your mind, will, and emotions)* must be transformed by renewing your mind through the Word of God *(Romans 12:2)*.

You must begin to search your heart and *identify* the beliefs, or bad seeds, that are associated with trauma, that need to be "uprooted".

When these beliefs are revealed, you cannot continue to leave them "buried" if you really want to be free.

You must acknowledge truth, for it is only truth that will set you free.

Scripture admonishes us to confess our sins one to another so that we may be healed. Hiding behind and confessing a lie won't help you attain healing.

The Bible also states that the heart is deceitful above all things and desperately wicked – who can know it? Well, God does.

So, you must ask God to show you what's in your heart. Say aloud, "Lord, show me the areas of my heart and soul that need to be healed!"

As it was with the woman at the well, *(John 4)* I believe you will be confronted with TRUTH during this journey.

Not just *your* truth – but *the* truth!

Your truth can differ from *the* truth! And it's alright that the two may differ because it speaks to where you are mentally and emotionally in regard to a matter. However, God wants you to be able to face and accept *the* truth.

Understanding and believing truth will create a pathway to help facilitate healing and allow you the freedom to flourish!

STRONGHOLDS

When your soul has been wounded or traumatized, that trauma is generally a gateway for the "enemy of your soul", Satan, *(Ephesians 6:10-12 and Psalm 143:3)* or other demonic spirits, to enter in and "take root", or to build a negative stronghold".

The word stronghold is defined as the following:

1. *A place that has been fortified so as to protect against attack.*

2. *A place where a particular cause or belief is strongly defended or upheld.*

Strongholds can be positive or negative. First, let's examine a positive stronghold.

Psalm 27: 1
Adonai is my light and salvation; whom do I need to fear? Adonai is the stronghold of my life: of whom should I be afraid?

This scripture assures us that God, himself, is the stronghold of our lives. He is our place of fortification and our protection against attack. In addition, He and the totality of His Word, *(including what He says about us)*, are the strongholds that should be built in our hearts.

These are the truths and beliefs that are worthy of being defended and upheld.

Now, let's take a look at strongholds of the enemy.

2 Corinthians 10:3-5

3 For although we do live in the world, we do not wage war in a worldly way; 4 because the weapons we use to wage war are not worldly. On the contrary, they have God's power for demolishing strongholds. We demolish arguments 5 and every arrogance that raises itself up against the knowledge of God; we take every thought captive and make it obey the Messiah.

If the scripture is admonishing us to pull down a stronghold, you better believe that God did not build it!

Remember that strongholds are *places of protection and places where our beliefs are upheld.* There are indeed spiritual strongholds, or wrong beliefs, that our spiritual weapons of the word, prayer, fasting, etc. have the power to destroy.

The key to understanding my point is understanding the next part of the scripture about "casting down arguments" and "bringing your thoughts into captivity."

By this, we see that strongholds are built in your mind and heart through words – yours or someone else's.

Therefore, we must destroy any thought, whether from other people or ourselves, that goes against the word of God and what He has spoken about us.

WHAT SEEDS HAVE SHAPED YOU?

A stronghold is not only a part of your belief system, but it is attached to the very spirit in which your belief system lies. This is either the Spirit of God, or the spirit of fear, which is from the enemy.

According to John 10:10, Jesus states, "The thief (Satan) comes only to steal, kill and destroy; I came that they may have life and have it in abundance."

Jesus is speaking about quality of life. He came to give life; Satan comes to take it away. How does he accomplish this? Generally, by taking advantage of the traumatic, negative experiences of your life and using them to keep you mentally bound to a negative, emotional effect.

The result of negative experiences often manifests in a lie within your mind.

For example, you may have been abandoned as a child and you believe in your mind that no one will ever "want" you. While the experience is true, the belief resulting from the experience is a lie.

If we believe a lie is the truth, we may remain in a constant battle within ourselves until that battle is resolved.

This is one reason you may start projects, but don't complete them.

Perhaps you know that part of your destiny is to be in the forefront or in the spotlight, yet you also feel like you don't want to be seen. It's likely that there is a stronghold in your mind developed from a bad seed and it's fighting to keep you within its walls.

Bad seeds can cause you to live in a state of confusion about your identity and purpose. You become double-minded about what you know God is calling you to do, versus the actions that you take to accomplish it.

One day you want to start a business or ministry and the next day… just thinking about it gives you a headache… literally!

Maybe God has instructed you to write a book, but you think to yourself, "I can't share my story – people will think I'm weird."

Perhaps you desire to be married, yet you keep thinking about the hurt that the last relationship caused you, so you choose not to trust anyone.

Do you have a gift you want to share with the world, but you don't because you were hurt by a negative comment about your gift?

We want to uncover the seeds within you that cause instability and double-mindedness to manifest.

Please say this prayer aloud...

Father,
You are the Sovereign God who reigns on the throne. All power belongs to you. You know my heart. As I prepare to go forward in this journey, I'm asking that You uncover, uproot, heal, and restore all areas of my heart and mind that need it! In Jesus' name, amen.

First, I want you to list any negative beliefs that have become a stronghold for you. Thoughts that you believe could keep you from advancing in life. *(i.e. No one likes me; I'm not smart; etc.)*

_____
_____
_____
_____
_____
_____
_____
_____

Next, list any desires or dreams for your life that you are double-minded about. *(i.e. I want to be a singer, but I'm afraid to sing in front of people.)*

_____
_____
_____
_____
_____
_____
_____
_____

With regard to what you have written above (for both) what do you think would happen if you allowed those strongholds and fears to stop you from moving forward and how would you feel?

_____
_____
_____
_____
_____
_____
_____
_____
_____

What do you think would happen if you overcame the strongholds and fears and how would you feel?

_____
_____
_____
_____
_____
_____
_____
_____
_____
_____
_____
_____
_____
_____
_____
_____
_____
_____
_____
_____
_____
_____
_____

Chapter 2

Walking Wilted

Psalm 91:4-5…He will cover you with his pinions, and under his wings you will find refuge; his truth is a shield and protection. 5 You will not fear the terrors of night or the arrow that flies by day…

When flowers don't get the kind of nourishment they need to thrive, they are prone to wilting. Wilting can be caused by bacteria, fungus, lack of water, air in the stems, or other detriments. If not remedied, these can lead to the slow death of the flower.

If you have experienced any type of trauma, and we all have on some level, until you are healed, you live with the consequences, or manifestations of that trauma. As a result, we can "walk wilted".

Walking wilted can take on the form of several issues.

For example, out of molestation can come gender dysphoria, promiscuity, pornography, addiction, depression, etc.

If you have experienced rejection or abandonment, you may build walls in relationships so that you cannot be "hurt" or rejected again. Perhaps even worse, you might continue to seek acceptance from those who rejected you.

Out of hurt, can grow anger, rage, and if left unchecked, even a murderous spirit can take root inside of us.

Everyone responds to trauma differently. Though, once our eyes are opened to it, it is up to us to seek the help we need to become fully healed.

Let's say a quick prayer as we go a bit deeper...

Father,
In Jesus' name, I come before You, open in heart and spirit. May Your light shine brightly into the dark places of my heart and expose all that is not like You. I desire to be healed, whole, and transformed in body, mind, and spirit.

Show me the root of anything holding me back! Show me the areas of my mind that need to be renewed! Holy Spirit lead me and guide me into all truth about myself. In Jesus' name, amen!

OUCH!
I DIDN'T KNOW THAT WAS THERE!

It can be hard to "see" yourself. What you call "protecting" yourself, could really be a manifestation from a wound of being rejected.

You may think you are just a quiet or shy person, but you could have a fear of people and what they will say about you.

Wounds are often invisible to us but they can be quite clear to those around us.

How can you recognize if you are wounded? Two words... YOUR REACTIONS.

When you are involved in a situation, and you react harshly and experience strong negative feelings, if those feelings and reactions are inappropriate and "over-the-top" within the situation, more than likely you are wounded.

For example, if you get angry with your friend because she ventures beyond the invisible boundaries you've assigned to her by becoming friends with someone you don't like, is the kind of anger that you feel warranted? If feelings of jealousy arise and you display out-of-control behavior toward your friend, you must ask yourself why are you so angry; why do you feel jealous; and why do you feel the need to control your friend?

Perhaps your significant other forgets to call you during work hours and when he gets home you accuse him of cheating. Barring that he hasn't given you a legitimate reason not to trust him, you must ask yourself why do you have feelings of distrust and where did they come from?

I remember a friend telling me that their spouse got extremely angry because they forgot to eat the dinner that the spouse left in the refrigerator. Why would something like that trigger such a reaction?

Maybe you feel extremely hurt because a friend jokingly calls you lazy, and emotionally you descend into sadness and depression. Why would that word trigger those emotions for you?

In the next space, write down a situation where your reaction may have been unwarranted for the situation.

_____

_____

_____

_____

_____

_____

_____

_____

Why do you think you reacted that way? Be honest with yourself.

_____

_____

_____

_____

_____

_____

_____

Remember—Inappropriate reactions can be a result of wounds in our soul that were never healed.

HOW WOUNDS ARE PROJECTED

Our senses are used as gateways to inflict wounds in the soul. Things we see, hear, feel, experience, even taste and smell, can affect the way we think, our beliefs and values, as well as the condition of our heart and emotions.

Wounds are generally projected in two ways… through experiences and words.

Let's focus on experiences first.

EXPERIENCES

An experience is defined as a particular instance of personally encountering or undergoing something.

The kind of experience I am referring to can be direct, physically traumatic events like molestation, rape, physical abuse, life-changing accidents, etc., as well as other mentally traumatic experiences.

Events like witnessing abuse in the home as a child, the death of a loved one at an early age or being rejected or treated differently by a loved one or your peers.

In most instances, wounds can go unnoticed *(as in my case)* for many years, and go unhealed because we think we don't need help for them, or we are afraid to seek help because of the stigma attached to the experience that caused them.

Regardless, as with ALL wounds, without proper healing, they become infected and can infect the entire area around it. This is when the "wilt" becomes a slow death.

Now, let's look at how words can affect us.

WORDS

Words can be beautiful, encouraging, delightful, exciting, and edifying, but they can also be hurtful, cruel, negative, and even physically painful.

What we hear and receive into our spirit is so important because words literally have the power to shape our world and us. Let me share a familiar passage of scripture with you...

Proverbs 18:21 (The Message Bible)
Words kill, words give life; they're either poison or fruit—you choose.

I think we can all agree that words can give life, but did you know that words can kill?

How? By inflicting wounds in our soul. Hurtful words are often depicted in the Bible as sharp objects such as arrows and swords.

Psalm 64:4-5 (3-4 in most translations)
4 They sharpen their tongues like a sword; they aim their arrows, poisoned words, 5 in order to shoot from cover at the innocent, shooting suddenly and fearing nothing.

Psalm 55:22 (21 in most translations)
What he said sounded smoother than butter, but his heart was at war. His words seemed more soothing than oil, but in fact they were sharp swords.

While the scriptures are metaphorical in nature, they are actually describing what's happening in the spirit realm when negative words are used.

Has someone ever spoken words to you that felt like a literal dagger in your heart? I have.

Your heart can be wounded by the hurtful words of another, unless you are properly covered using the shield of faith which is a part of the full armor of God listed in Ephesians 6:14-16.

The bible exclaims that it is the shield of faith (or trust) "that quenches every FIERY DART of the enemy".

Psalm 28:7 declares that *"ADONAI* is my strength and **shield**; in Him my heart trusted, and I have been helped. Therefore my heart is filled with joy, and I will sing praises to Him."

So you see it is the Lord, Himself, who is our shield and the One who can protect our hearts. Of course, this truth often takes maturity and understanding to become useful for us.

I would venture to say that many of us were unaware of the full armor of God as young people and I would add to that we are generally ill-equipped in using the armor in adulthood as well.

I remember praying for a woman that was dealing with a spirit of guilt over a situation with her mother. To illustrate how she felt, she made a movement with her hands as if she was stabbing herself in the chest.

On reflex, I reached toward her chest, grabbed the invisible dagger and pulled it out! Immediately, we both felt the anointing of God! It was as if a natural dagger had been pulled from her chest.

We prayed more extensively later, and God healed her completely! He lifted the burden *(which manifested in shoulder and back pain)* and delivered her from guilt.

I know that God desires to heal you as well! I'm praying that God is revealing more to you about the wounds of your soul as you are reading. Record any additional thoughts or revelations here.

_____
_____
_____
_____
_____
_____
_____
_____
_____
_____
_____
_____
_____
_____
_____
_____
_____

Chapter 3

The Master Gardener and You

Song of Solomon 4:16 Awake, north wind, and come, south wind! Blow on my garden, that its fragrance may spread everywhere. Let my beloved come into his garden and taste its choice fruits.

To blossom into the beautiful and unique flower that you are created to be takes time. When growing a flower, there are steps to consider, and each step is an integral part of the flower's development. One must consider the planting, germination process, nutrients in the soil, how much water it needs, and the amount of light it should receive. However, one of the most important considerations that we don't often think about is the skill level of the gardener.

Is the person "tending to you" a beginner or are they advanced in their knowledge of how to care for you?

God is the Master Gardener! He created you. He knows what you are supposed to "look like"! Your petals should be a certain color … your leaves should be healthy… your stem should be strong … and you should attract those to whom you are called to in a certain way.

In other words, your unique beauty and purpose should resonate with and be fruitful to you and to those who are divinely connected to you. Only a Master Gardener can nurture you to a healthy, FULL BLOOM!

THE SEARCH FOR SOMETHING BEAUTIFUL

You cannot control where you are born, the family to which you are born, or the environment in which you grow up. These factors surely contribute to our identity, positive or negative. However, as we grow, mature, and trust God to reveal our identity in Him, we come to realize that as Romans 8:28 declares…

All things work together for the good of them that love God and are called according to His purpose.

You may wonder why you had to endure certain events. My first Pastor, Bishop Dale C. Bronner, a wonderfully wise man, frenquently states, "Everything is God sent or God used."

I believe his statement.

If we love God, there is an exchange of "beauty for ashes". I believe the situations in our lives that we deem to be "negative" can somehow work together for the good and bring glory to God.

The childhood trauma of losing my Mother became the basis of my search for identity. Today, one of my gifts and deepest passions is to empower others in their search.

The breakup you went through probably taught you a lot about yourself and what you really need in a relationship versus what's been familiar to you.

The abuse that you endured surfaced a kind of courage and resiliency that you didn't know you possessed!

What didn't kill you not only made you stronger but gave you the wisdom and insight to help others in similar situations.

When your relationship with God is strong, your perspective of life can't help but change. You begin to see yourself, other people, and situations in a different way.

THE GARDENER'S WAY

The Gardener has a way of "wooing" you. I remember a dream the Lord gave me during my first year with Him.

In the dream, I quietly observed a man, maybe about five yards from me, tending a garden. He slowly turned toward my right diagonal, walked away and smiled at me as if to say, "Go have a look."

Timidly stepping forward, I realized it was a fruit garden. The beauty and the size of the fruit were astonishing! My eyes were immediately drawn to the largest apple I'd ever seen *(maybe the size of a soccer ball)* and it was the most amazing and vibrant color of red.

In fact, all of the fruit, as well as the leaves, were so vibrant that it was as if the garden was alive!

When I woke up, I knew the gardener was God and the fruit was reflective of the kind of "fruit" he desired to produce in my life.

I am brought to tears as I write this remembering the gentleness of the spirit of "The Gardener" and how He walked away to allow me the "space" I needed to come forward.

I didn't feel the pressure of someone "looking over my shoulder" as I browsed the garden.

The Father is truly a gentleman.

As you come forward with the matters of your heart, the strongholds, the wounds of your soul... all of the things that leave you "walking wilted", I believe He will give you the "space" that you need to deal with each issue. He knows what you are ready to handle, and he also knows the cry of your heart.

A PECULIAR PROCESS

Everyone's process with The Gardener is different. However, as you move forward, please be aware of any feelings of resistance that start to arise. As much as you desire to be healed, sometimes your subconscious mind, the strongholds you have built, AND the "enemy of your soul" will attempt to distract, deter, and discourage you!

I encourage you to stay focused on your total healing and visualize what that would look like for you.

One more thing… remember this —

Freedom within comes from a strong desire to obtain it!

Chapter 4

Uprooting

Matthew 15:13 He replied, "Every plant that my Father in heaven has not planted will be pulled up by the roots."

So far, we have been tilling the ground of your heart. Certain memories are being "turned over" and perhaps God is even bringing repressed ones to the surface. I pray that God will reveal everything to you that is needed for your complete healing.

Now begins the uprooting process.

When people have sown negative seeds into you, in many cases, the seed is cyclical. Meaning, it's a seed that was sown into them or a seed that has been sown generationally.

This is one reason you see patterns of alcoholism, abuse, drug addiction, pornography, incest, molestation, etc. in families.

The Bible says that people perish for a lack of knowledge. In our own ignorance, we say and do things to our family members and to others that are ungodly and unrighteous. We pay the price for such ignorance.

Our words and actions are generally manifestations of our own experiences and until you can face your bad experiences and be healed, you are prone to becoming a bad experience for someone else.

ARE YOU READY?

The following is a quote from the website, Quora…

"The root system of a plant is, generally speaking, the heart of its circulatory system… You uproot it, it typically dies."

The bad seeds *(the negative experiences and words)* must be uprooted and die in order for you to move forward effectively and LIVE!

The word of God declares that to everything there is a time and season... a time to plant and a time to uproot! Now is your time!

THE MIRACLE TOOL OF FORGIVENESS

Forgiveness is God's divine garden tool that plows deep in the heart! It will uproot every negative seed that has ever been sown into your life. It facilitates the truest form of healing.

Sometimes forgiveness is the most difficult process to undergo. Why? Because it requires you to tear down the very stronghold that you have built up for your "protection".

The irony of this is instead of the stronghold protecting you, it imprisons your feelings of anger, bitterness, resentment, hurt, shame, guilt, _____, etc... *(you fill in the blank)* and keeps them chained to your heart!

My beloved sister, this is not God's desire for you!

You may not even realize that you harbor unforgiveness. As it was in my case, it can hide deep within your heart.

As a result of allowing unforgiveness to "take root", we have let many "suns" *(days)* go down while angry and have built a stronghold.

Ephesians 4:26
Be angry, but don't sin — don't let the sun go down before you have dealt with the cause of your anger...

Matthew 6:14
For if you forgive others their offenses, your heavenly Father will also forgive you...

Forgiveness is not a "natural" endeavor. While it's a relatively simple concept, it can be an extremely layered and complex.

Have your ever been angry with someone, then decided to forgive them? Yet, when you saw them again, you could feel the anger resurface?

You were probably able to peel back a few layers toward forgiving them, but you didn't quite get to the root of the anger. Again, your reaction will speak and not lie.

Forgiveness is like salvation in that it is a two-part process. First, it happens in the mind and we "confess" it.

We think about it, we're aware that it's the right thing to do, and we say to ourselves (and others), "I forgive them."

However, Romans 10:9 gives us the "key" to the second part. It says, "… that if you confess with your mouth that Jesus is Lord and believe in your heart that God raised him from the dead, you shall be saved."

Salvation is a two-part work! It requires confessing the Lord Jesus and believing in His resurrection!

Resurrection is bringing something to life that was once dead. It's revived, renewed, and restored! That which was dead appears as though it had never died.

Forgiveness requires the same type of work! You must be able to confess it with your mouth *(to yourself and others)* and believe it in your heart.

It is the belief in your heart that completes the work!

The part of your heart that was dead because of what you went through is brought back to life through complete forgiveness.

When this occurs, you can talk *about* the person or even talk *with* the person, and no longer be affected by the wounds or bound by the stronghold. You just might find yourself loving them with the love of Christ because you are able to view them *through* the love of Christ. Now, that's another level of love, my friend! (Even though it may be from afar♥)

SPEAKING OF LOVE...

1 John 4:18
There is no fear in love. On the contrary, love that has achieved its goal gets rid of fear, because fear has to do with punishment; the person who keeps fearing has not been brought to maturity in regard to love.

Fear is the driving force behind strongholds and fuels the desire to remain in unforgiveness.

Again, the stronghold that has been built is the "place of protection" and it can be frightening to tear it down. It can make you feel vulnerable to being hurt again.

However, the more we live in a place of fear, which is of the enemy, the more the stronghold is reinforced.

The Bible says that God is love and that perfect love casts out fear.

Forgiveness allows for love to enter in, and love allows for "replanting".

Once you have honestly forgiven, the Holy Spirit can fill that place in your heart and your capacity to love is enlarged.

MY TESTIMONY... CONTINUED

As we've previously discussed, we must be transformed by renewing our minds! Remember our minds are a part of our soul and the soul houses the mind, will, and emotions.

Through the death of my mother, repressed feelings of anger and abandonment were allowed to take root and the way was made for the enemy to occupy a place in my heart.

Although I had been a believer and servant of God for years, these spirits remained with me until my time of freedom!

As I explained before, my birth mother was killed when I was very young.

Because I never talked about it, nor received healing, the trauma from that tragedy was buried so deep inside of me, that I didn't even know I carried it... until one day...

THE MARRIAGES

My second marriage was a part of my "belly of the whale" experience. *(Refer to the book of Jonah in the Bible.)* I was running from my God-given assignment and ran right into trouble.

But first things first, let's start at the beginning...

My first marriage was the first for both of us and while we had much to learn about being married, I believed that we could make it. The challenges we had weren't what I deemed to be "serious" and I was willing.

Being transparent, I would say it took about six months of living together to get out of the mindset of being "independent"; to understand that I didn't have to take care of everything myself.

I desired to display this from the beginning but renewing my mind to the idea was a process.

However, at the end of six months, he announced to me, "I'm not in love with you anymore" and that he was filing for divorce.

Of course, this was devastating to my heart. I knew that this was a God-ordained marriage and I will always stand by that statement.

Nonetheless, even when something is ordained by God, always remember that people have a choice. Even God doesn't "make" us love and obey Him. We love, honor and worship Him… by choice.

Shortly after my former husband made this announcement, he told me that God spoke to him and lead him to the scripture below…

Malachi 2:13-14

13 Here is something else you do: you cover Adonai's altar with tears, with weeping and with sighing, because he no longer looks at the offering or receives your gift with favor. 14 Nevertheless, you ask, "Why is this?" Because Adonai is witness between you and the wife of your youth that you have broken faith with her, though she is your companion, your wife by covenant.

When he shared this with me, I knew that God was indeed speaking to him about us, yet not many months later, he made his decision to leave.

Even after the divorce, the Lord told me that He was still speaking to him, but after a period of time, God eventually showed me that my former husband had "chosen to go his *own way.*"

The Bible says that there is a way that *seems right* to a man, and it also says that we are led away by the desires of our own heart. This is why it's important that we ask God to reveal what's in our heart and in what areas does our mind need to be renewed. We want to be led by the Spirit, not our flesh.

Over the years, he has apologized to me a few times and I to him. With a humble heart, he told me he was being selfish at the time and asked for my forgiveness.

Actually, I thought I had forgiven him prior to him even asking, but upon seeing him one day, the reaction of my heart told me that the root of unforgiveness was still there.

Once I realized this, I asked a friend, an Apostle in ministry, to pray with me. During the prayer, I could hear the Lord asking me to give it to Him. I saw myself holding onto this "thing" in my heart. It was like God was asking me for my "security blanket" and I didn't want to give it to Him.

I didn't know that I felt this way, or even saw the unforgiveness as "security". My flesh didn't want to let it go, but my spirit knew and believed that God only wanted what was best for me, and it was best to let it go. I made the sincere choice to do just that.

As I "released" it, I could feel it uprooting, I could see God taking it, and I felt joyous in the process!

The next time I saw him, I knew that the miracle of forgiveness had truly set me free. How did I know? My reaction to him and what I felt in my heart!

There was no bitterness, no resentment, and no anger! On the contrary, I saw him as my brother in Christ and could genuinely desire God's best for him! It was a wonderful feeling and it has lasted until today! Praise God!

THE DISCOVERY

Seven years later, I married someone that I had much in common with creatively. We even shared an entrepreneurial spirit.

He was a believer, an altar worker in church, and could generally be described as a "great guy" with great qualities… and I would say the same.

However, he was also a verbally abusive man, who not only had deep wounds from being abandoned by his father at twelve years old, but I believe also suffered from Post-Traumatic Stress Disorder, or PTSD. In fact, he even wrote a children's book on the subject, from a child's point of view.

His abusive behavior would manifest in different ways.

In him, I would see manifestations of anger, rage, criticism, and judgement. Manipulation and control were especially prevalent. In the church, we call this a "Jezebel spirit". *(Refer to the story of Jezebel in 1 and 2 Kings)* Spirits are not gender-based. They can affect anyone.

He displayed text-book abusive behavior with spiritual manifestations of the issues of his heart and the wounds of his soul; wounds that included rejection, insecurity, fear, shame, and guilt.

There is always a reason for someone's behavior. You just have to look deep enough to uncover the roots.

Let me continue…

In order to try to exert control over me, or "punish" me, he would "take things" from me.

For example, he would take back gifts he had given to me, cancel planned activities, or would even take his voice from me by not speaking to me for days, sometimes weeks. While this was frustrating at times, the "punishment" never triggered anger in me because those things were not that important to me.

One fateful day though, he was angry with me about something, and he took the external drive attached to my computer. As a graphic designer, this drive was important to me. It not only contained the work of my hands, my creativity, but it contained all of the work files for my clients.

When he took it, an anger arose in me that I'd never felt before. He refused to return it to me, and I shouted the words "I hate you!"

Later, after calming down and being in a place where I could think more clearly, I became increasingly aware that this anger didn't feel "normal" to me.

I asked myself, and God, questions … Why did I get so angry at him for taking the drive? Nothing else he took or did made me *that* angry… why this? Why did this action trigger a reaction strong enough for me to say, "I hate you"?

I was desperate for answers. Instinctively, I knew that it felt like I had a "spirit of anger", which is NOT of God and I didn't want ANY part of it.

During the process of seeking God for answers, He gave me the revelation that the anger arose when something I deemed "important" was "taken from me". Ah-ha! What a valuable discovery for me!

My friend, within a couple of days, God gave me a dream that showed me the anger was connected to my birth mother.

A few days later, this was confirmed by a prophet who spoke of the "event that happened when you were around three years old" and that "God was going to deal with it quickly".

Just two days later, my time of freedom arrived… and in the least likely place, or so I thought. *(Now I understand that there was even purpose in the place!)*

I went to see a film, in which Eddie Murphy starred, called "A Thousand Words". Eddie's character was not the nicest man and used his words carelessly. He was given a special tree in his backyard and for every word he spoke, a leaf fell from the tree. When he realizes this, he tries to be more careful with his words.

And Then I Started Feeling Pretty

During most of the movie, the audience is led to believe that he is angry because his father left him
and his mother when he was a child. Later, we find out that his father had died!

I cannot put into words what my heart felt when this is revealed. Near the end of the movie, he uses his last three words, kneeling at his father's grave, to say, "I forgive you."

Every emotion in me bubbled to the surface! With great effort, I tried to control my emotions during the movie, but I couldn't stop the tears from breaking through.

When the movie was finally over, I rushed to my car feeling as if a dam were about to break inside of me.

Barely making it inside of my car, the dam broke and I began crying uncontrollably!

In a rush of emotions, I forgave my birth mother, Linda for dying… for "leaving me"… for "abandoning" me. I forgave God for "taking her", and even as I was saying it, I knew it wasn't necessarily "biblical", but that's how I felt and that's what came out.

Next, I asked my mother for forgiveness for harboring the buried anger that I held against her, and I asked God to forgive me for the blame and anger I felt towards Him.

Then suddenly, from the depths of my soul, I leaned over toward the passenger seat and released two of the deepest, gut-wrenching screams that have ever come out of my mouth.

It didn't even "sound" like me! I was keenly aware that a spirit was leaving me with each scream.

INSTANTLY…I FELT DIFFERENT.

(The Bible describes physical manifestations of convulsing and shouting when spirits are being expelled. Refer to the work of Jesus and the New Testament!)

I knew something supernatural occurred. I felt lighter and happier. I felt an inner peace I'd never known before.

I said to myself, "I think I just got delivered! Lord, did I just get delivered?"

And I heard the Lord say, "Anger and abandonment."

"Oh my gosh! I can't believe it," I thought to myself! I just got set free sitting in my car, no one laying

And Then I Started Feeling Pretty

hands on me, but by the SPIRIT OF THE LIVING GOD!

Immediately, I asked God to fill the places that anger and abandonment once occupied in my heart; to fill it with His love and with the Holy Spirit. I literally felt an infilling occur!

To "test" if my newfound freedom was real, I purposely didn't tell my *(then)* husband what happened.

We had arranged to meet at a coffee shop a few days later. As I waited for him, I looked at the people in the store. I felt a love for them that I had never felt before! I wanted to go outside and shout to the world, "I LOVE YOU!"

When he arrived, we sat and talked. He looked at me peculiar, but never said anything.

Later that evening, he said to me, "You seem different. What happened to you?"

I shared my story with him.

There is no doubt within me that God truly and supernaturally delivered me! All glory and praise to God!

I have been able to forgive him and let go and I pray that he forgives me as well. I declare God's best for him and that he fulfills the will of God for his life.

LESSONS LEARNED

I realized that I had developed a stronghold in my subconscious that caused me to react fiercely at what I felt was a violation to me; "taking" something from me that I viewed as meaningful and important.

I find it sobering to know that I walked around for 40 years with spirits of anger and abandonment without realizing it.

Looking back, I believe I felt that same anger after my first divorce, I just wasn't mature enough then to connect it to the wound of my soul.

Even more sobering to me is the fact that I had been walking with God for eighteen years, (thirteen years in ministry), baptized with the Holy Spirit, anointed, and trying to follow God's will, yet I was still "walking wilted" and bound in my soul.

The fact is that most of us would like to believe that we become whole after receiving Christ. The reality is your spirit *is* made new, but you still need to be healed in your soul!

Again, I believe everything is God sent or God used.

God used this hurtful time in my life not only to free me from my own deepest hurt, but it also developed a passion in me for women that are affected by abuse and domestic violence.

Actually, the experience of it opened my eyes to the fact that I lost my birth mother to domestic violence and helped me to understand aspects of my calling in this area.

GET YOUR TOOLS AND LET'S DIG!

Alright, take a deep breath…and if you are ready to move forward, go back and look at pages 32, 33, 39, and 44. Think about the words you have heard and the experiences that you've had that have resulted in wounds of your soul.

On the lines below, I want you to write down the person, or persons, names that have caused a wound in your soul.

Then, write down what they spoke to you or what they did to you to cause the wound. If you do not know the name or names, then just record the event.

Whether or not they intended to wound you, whether or not they were aware of their words or actions, and whether or not they have apologized for the wound is not the most important factor.

The most important factor is that you confess it to God and forgive them in your heart.

Name/s_____

_____
_____
_____
_____
_____

Name/s_____

_____
_____
_____
_____
_____

And Then I Started Feeling Pretty

Name/s_____

_____
_____
_____
_____
_____
_____
_____

Name/s_____

_____
_____
_____
_____
_____
_____
_____

If you need more space, please use a notebook that is used specifically for chronicling this journey of forgiveness and healing.

Take your time and pray the following prayer aloud and follow the flow of your spirit.

May all things be revealed and healed, in Jesus' name!

And remember this… you must be honest with yourself. If it's not truly in your heart to forgive and repent for harboring unforgiveness, it's best to wait until you can do it with a sincere heart. Just continue to ask God for help.

PRAYER OF FREEDOM AND FORGIVENESS

Father,
In Jesus name, I come humbly before You, seeking Your face, honoring and acknowledging You in all things. You are my Beginning and End. You are the Author and Completer of my faith. I take comfort in knowing that Your Word says that You know the plans You have for me; plans for my well-being, not for bad things; so that I can have hope and a future. You said if I call to You, You will listen to me, and when I seek You with my whole heart, I will find You.

Your Word says that Jesus came to bind the brokenhearted and to set the captive free! Right now, Lord, I'm seeking You for the healing of my heart and for freedom in my soul.

According to Luke 10:19, I take authority over every negative seed, every negative word that has been spoken over me, and every negative experience that my heart holds hostage.

I cast down every vain imagination that has exalted itself, in my life, against the knowledge of God.

I declare and decree the lies of the enemy no longer have any power over me… spirit, soul, or body! I speak healing in my heart!

I rebuke and uproot every negative seed that has resulted in self-hatred, self-pity, self-denial, self-destruction, self-sabotage, self-centeredness, pride, fear, anger, bitterness, hurt, rage, insecurity, jealousy, guilt, shame, _____ *(add anything else that comes to your spirit)* and unforgiveness!

(As you read the next part below, take your time and allow the Spirit of God to minister to you. Wait until you feel a release before moving to the next person or event.)

*Lord, I forgive _____(name) and release them in my heart for _____(what they did). *(*refer to pages 70 and 71)*

Father,
I repent and ask You for forgiveness for harboring toxic emotions and allowing them to reside in my heart. I thank you that You are faithful to forgive, as we forgive others and ask for forgiveness.

Holy Spirit fill up every place in my heart where anything that is not like You once resided.

Fill my heart with Your love! Fill my heart with more fruit of the Spirit. Fill my heart with mercy, grace, and forgiveness!

Thank You for loving me with perfect love. Thank you for showing me and teaching me that Your ways are perfect. In Jesus' name! Amen!

And Then I Started Feeling Pretty

Notes:

And Then I Started Feeling Pretty

Notes:_____
_____
_____
_____
_____
_____
_____
_____
_____
_____
_____
_____
_____
_____
_____
_____
_____
_____
_____
_____
_____
_____
_____
_____
_____
_____
_____
_____
_____

Chapter 5

Replanting

Romans 1:2 In other words, do not let yourselves be conformed to the standards of the world. Instead, keep letting yourselves be transformed by the renewing of your minds; so that you will know what God wants and will agree that what He wants is good, satisfying, and able to succeed.

The Father speaks this to you...
"I've created you...your mind, your spirit, your very being for purpose. There is no other soul living that can take your place in what I've designed you to do. My people may have similar gifts, similar callings, and even similar styles, but just as your fingerprint is unique to you, you are unique to Me. No one can take your place in My kingdom."

A major step after receiving any type of healing or breakthrough is having the tools and awareness to maintain it. This must be done intentionally.

GOOD SEEDS AND A NEW MIND

After the bad seeds and roots are uprooted, it's time to sow new seeds! This is an exciting process that takes a bit of work, but if you are willing, you will reap a blessed harvest!

In essence, replanting is renewing the mind.

Why do we need to renew the mind?

As the word states in the scripture under the chapter heading, Romans 1:2, the purpose of renewing the mind is so that we will know what God wants and will agree that what He wants is good, satisfying, and able to succeed.

Desiring the complete will of God takes a renewed mind! We are selfish by nature… we want what WE want!

To allow the Lord to lead you and believe that He wants and knows what's best for you takes a different perspective and trust.

The beautiful thing is that His Word promises that when you delight yourself in Him, He will give you the desires of your heart.

The more you spend time with God, worshipping Him and reading His Word, the more He speaks to your heart. And as this happens… what HE wants eventually becomes what YOU want.

That being said, understand that you are born with purpose. So, if you have always seen yourself owning a business, becoming an actress, being a great motivational speaker or a _____ *(you fill in the blank)*, please believe that desire is in your heart for a reason.

Also, remember that His Word says that He can do ABOVE all that you can ask or think! When you surrender your life to Him and let Him lead, He will take you places you never would have thought about – even within the realm of your purpose!

YOUR ASSIGNMENT

I want to help you renew your mind in two areas, understanding who God is, and understanding who you are in Him.

I'm going to list ten scriptures and what I call a brief "point of meditation" or P.O.M. for each.

Please read them all aloud and meditate on them for the next thirty days. Ask God to give you revelation as you meditate on them and visually see them being "planted" in your heart.

WHO IS GOD?

Before I list the scriptures, indulge me a moment as I talk about our Father... The Master Gardener!

There are several names for God in the Hebrew language that describes His nature and who He is. Below are just a few...

Jehovah Jireh	God is Provider
Jehovah El Roi	The God Who Sees
El Shaddai	God the Almighty
Jehovah Shalom	God is Peace

I bear witness to all of these within my personal life. However, perhaps the characteristic I am most familiar with is...

Jehovah Pelet   The Lord is my Deliverer

Yes indeed! He has truly been my Deliverer!

He has also been my Father, my Peace, my Courage, my Friend, my Confidant, my Counselor, my Comfort, my Joy, my Strength, my Honor, my Righteous Judge, my Teacher, my Revelation, my Victory, my Transformation, my Coach, my Partner, my Husband, my Praise, my Worship, my Creativity, my Love…my Everything!

I love Him and He loves me. Nothing and no one will ever change that, and NO ONE can ever take His place! Hallelujah!

Scriptures (good seeds) for meditation:

Genesis 1:1
In the beginning, God created the heavens and the earth.

> (P.O.M. – God existed before anything was created. He is eternal.)

John 3:16
For God so loved the world that He gave His only and unique Son, so that everyone who trusts in Him may have eternal life, instead of being utterly destroyed.

> (P.O.M. – God loves the world, including ME!)

Numbers 23:19
God is not a human who lies or a mortal who changes His mind. When he says something, He will do it; when He makes a promise, He will fulfill it.

> (P.O.M. – God is Faithful! I can count on Him to keep His promises.)

Psalm 34:20 (19 in most translations)
The righteous person suffers many evils, but Adonai rescues him out of them all.

> (P.O.M. – God will help me through affliction.)

1 Peter 5:7
Throw all your anxieties upon Him, because He cares about you.

>(P.O.M. – God cares about me.)

Isaiah 41:13
For I, *Adonai*, your God, say to you, as I hold your right hand, 'Have no fear; I will help you.

>(P.O.M. – God is always with me to strengthen me.)

Galatians 6:7
Don't delude yourselves: no one makes a fool of God! A person reaps what he sows.

>(P.O.M. – God sees everything.)

Jeremiah 32:27
Look, I am *Adonai*, the God of every living creature; is there anything too hard for Me?

>(P.O.M. – Nothing is too hard for God!)

Psalm 5:12 (11 in most translations)
But let all who take refuge in You rejoice, let them forever shout for joy! Shelter them; and they will be glad, those who love Your name.

(P.O.M. – God is my place of protection.)

Jeremiah 17:14
Heal me, LORD, and I will be healed; save me and I will be saved, for You are the one I praise.

> (P.O.M. – God will heal me, and God will save me.)

1 John 4:12
No one has ever seen God; if we love one another, God remains united with us, and our love for him has been brought to its goal in us.

> (P.O.M. – God is love and lives in me because I love.)

WHO ARE YOU?

I had a dream in which I saw a baby laying on my bed. (Babies generally mean something new in your life that you are responsible for… like a new project or ministry.) I picked up the baby and the rest went something like this…

Me: Oh my! Where did you come from? Who are you?
Baby: Who are you?'
Me: Noooo…Who are you?
Baby: No. Who are YOU?

As I was waking up, I heard a new song in my spirit that repeated the lyric, "Who do you want to be?"

Upon becoming fully awake, I knew, of course, that God was dealing with my mindset regarding my identity.

Below are a few questions for you to ponder and answer. As you answer them, keep in mind that as we are talking about identity, the focus is not who you are to other people, i.e. Wife, Mom, Aunt, etc., but who YOU are on the inside! Who did God create you to be?

For example, I am Alicia; Daughter of the Most High God. I am a Creator, Artist, and Visionary. I am a Teacher and Catalyst for Change. I am a Counselor and Defender of the People of God. I am an Architect; a

Builder of People. I am a Champion of Women… and yes, I am a Gardener.

If you need to think about a question, you can always return to it later, but please record the first thing that comes to mind.

Who are you?

_____
_____
_____
_____
_____
_____
_____

Who do you want to be?

_____
_____
_____
_____
_____
_____
_____

What do you believe God created you to do?

FACTS VS. LIES

Identity is defined as the <u>fact</u> of being who or what a person or thing is. So even by definition, identity has to do with facts, not lies.

The lie is "you don't matter".

The fact is "you have purpose"!

The lie is "nobody loves you".

The fact is "you are a child of God and no one could love you more!"

The lie is "it's over for you".

The fact is "it's not over until God says it is." *(And when He does, you'll be with Him.)*

The fact is that you are neither the negative or traumatic events that happened to you nor are you are the negative names someone called you.

You are who God says you are!

Interestingly, synonyms for identity include "oneness" and sameness".

As I stated before, everything is a product of its Maker. God says that He created you in His likeness and image! (Genesis 1:27).

God is your Maker. He is your Heavenly Father. You are "one" with Him. You are the "same" as He is, and because HE IS…YOU ARE!

God IS love, so you ARE **love**.

God IS joy, so you ARE **joy**.

God IS peace, so you ARE **peace**.

God IS creative, so you ARE **creative.**

God IS intelligent, so you ARE **intelligent.**

God IS prosperous, so you ARE **prosperous**.

God IS righteous, so you ARE **righteous.**

God IS holy, so you ARE **holy.**

The following scriptures declare who God says you are and His promises for your life.

The same assignment applies to these as the previous scriptures.

Speak them aloud and meditate on them for the next 30 days. Ask God to give you more revelation about who you are in Him!

Scriptures for meditation:

Genesis 1:27
So God created humankind in his own image; in the image of God he created him: male and female he created them.

> (P.O.M. – I am created in the image of God.)

John 1:12
But to as many as did receive him, to those who put their trust in his person and power, he gave the right to become children of God…

> (P.O.M. – I am a child of God.)

Jeremiah 1:5
Before I formed you in the womb, I knew you; before you were born, I separated you for myself. I have appointed you to be a prophet to the nations.

> (P.O.M. – God knew me before I was born and created me for purpose.)

1 Corinthians 12:27
Now you together constitute the body of the Messiah, and individually you are parts of it.

>(P.O.M. – I am a part of the body of Christ… the family of God.)

1 Peter 2:9
But you are a chosen people, the King's *cohanim (priesthood)*, a holy nation, a people for God to possess! Why? In order for you to declare the praises of the One who called you out of darkness into his wonderful light.

>(P.O.M. – I am chosen by God. I am a Queen…royalty; called into His light.)

1 Corinthians 6:19-20
Or don't you know that your body is a temple for the *Ruach HaKodesh (Holy Spirit)* who lives inside you, whom you received from God? The fact is, you don't belong to yourselves; for you were bought at a price. So use your bodies to glorify God.

>(P.O.M. – I am the temple of God's Spirit. He lives inside of me.)

Romans 6:6
We know that our old self was put to death on the execution-stake with Him, so that the entire body of our sinful propensities might be destroyed, and we might no longer be enslaved to sin.

(P.O.M. – I am a new creation in God.

Romans 8:1
Therefore, there is no longer any condemnation awaiting those who are in union with the Messiah Yeshua.

(P.O.M. – I am not condemned but will receive eternal life.)

Colossians 2:10
And it is in union with Him that you have been made full — He is the head of every rule and authority.

(POM – I am made complete in Christ.)

Ephesians 3:12
In union with Him, through His faithfulness, we have boldness and confidence when we approach God.

(P.O.M. – I have access to God through Christ.)

Romans 15:7
So welcome each other, just as the Messiah has welcomed you into God's glory.

(P.O.M. – I am accepted by Jesus.)

KEEP PLANTING

Psalm 139:13-15 For you fashioned my inmost being, you knit me together in my mother's womb. I thank you because I am awesomely made, wonderfully; your works are wonders – I know this very well.

As you embark upon the "replanting" process, I encourage you to delve into the Word more to find other scriptures that speak to the truth of who you are in the Lord.

I also encourage you to ask family and friends what they "see" in you. What are the positive traits and characteristics that they see in you that you may not see in yourself? I bet you may be surprised.

You are a WONDER… fearfully and wonderfully made as the Word declares!

The Hebrew word that is translated "fearfully" is *yare (Strongs #3372)*. It means "to be afraid, stand in awe, fear".

This isn't a fear that implies being scared, instead it implies honor, reverence and respect. .

Meaning, when God made you, He made you with reverence. He honors you, and He made you with respect.

When you "know this very well", in your heart, as the scripture above states, your view of yourself changes and the truth of this will begin to facilitate change around you!

REPLANTING TIP

I cannot emphasize it enough, if we are going to become the women God created us to be, we MUST change the way we think.

I like the translation of this scripture…

Romans 12:2 (New Living Translation)
Don't copy the behavior and customs of this world, but let God transform you into a new person by changing the way you think…

One of the changes I believe you can benefit from is to, as best you can, minimize "replaying" negative events that have already happened.

While it is natural to "replay" events, and if you are like me, you could play out a scenario over and over in your head of how things could have turned out, what you should have said, what they would have said if you said what you should have said, etc. (LOL)

This type of thinking is not beneficial. It can become condemning and damaging if you dwell on these kinds of thoughts too long.

If you are going to think on them, do your best to think about what can be learned from the situation, how you can grow, or how you can help someone else, then, move on. Do not allow guilt, shame, or condemnation to overtake your mind.

With practice, you can train your mind to think positive thoughts. You can live and think purposefully for today and look forward to tomorrow. This kind of thinking brings and keeps peace in your life.

Philippians 4:8-9
8 In conclusion, brothers, focus your thoughts on what is true, noble, righteous, pure, lovable or admirable, on some virtue or on something praiseworthy. 9 Keep doing what you have learned and received from me, what you have heard and seen me doing; then the God who gives shalom (peace) will be with you.

PRAYER FOR RENEWAL

Father,
You are truly the Master Gardener!
Hebrews 4:12 says, "See, the Word of God is alive! It is at work and is sharper than any double-edged sword — it cuts right through to where soul meets spirit and joints meet marrow, and it is quick to judge the inner reflections and attitudes of the heart." As I meditate on Your word and the truth about myself, continue to cut away and prune any reflections and attitudes of my heart that don't line up with Your word. Help me to receive Your truth. May it be planted deeply in my heart and change and transform my mind. Thank You for Your faithfulness! I'm so glad that Your Word endures forever! In Jesus' name! Amen!

And Then I Started Feeling Pretty

Notes:

And Then I Started Feeling Pretty

Notes:

Chapter 6

W.E.E.D.S.

2 Corinthians 10:5 Casting down imaginations and every high thing that exalts itself against the knowledge of God.

I stood in the attic, not quite sure what to expect. I was startled as four young men, pre-teen to teen-aged, burst boldly through the door. Each one approached me to fight. They were fairly easy to defeat, then there was a lull. I took advantage of the time to gather myself together.

While turned away from the door, I heard footsteps enter. It was a woman this time. I instantly knew that this would be, by far, the biggest challenge.

This was a dream I had many years ago, and the woman that walked through the door was me.

You are often your biggest battle! For years your subconscious mind has been trained to believe certain "truths".

The question is are these actual truths or are they lies that have kept you bound and stagnant?

W.E.E.D.S. IN THE GARDEN

During the process of renewing your mind from the initial "bad" seeds, other issues are sure to surface. I call these issues W.E.E.D.S. –**Wild Enchanted Enemies Determined to Stifle.**

W.E.E.D.S. are "vain imaginations" and are a part of the resistance I spoke of at the end of chapter three.

They are usually "random" internal thoughts that "pop up" in an effort to stifle your growth or can appear out of "nowhere" from external sources… sometimes from those that are closest to you.

They also can sound a lot like excuses!

I've found that the most common W.E.E.D.S. feed a root of fear.

THE FEAR FACTOR

Of the people that I have counseled over the years, I've found that most trauma results in a root of fear.

Fear is not from God.

2 Timothy 1:7
For God gave us a Spirit who produces not timidity, but power, love and self-discipline.

The Spirit of God produces the opposite of fear! Power is yours! Love is yours! Self-discipline is yours!

God encourages not to fear, but to be of good courage many times in the bible.

You must identify how fear manifests itself in your life before you can overcome it. It often hides… and the result of the W.E.E.D.S. it produces can often sound like the following:

False Humility
I just like to help everyone else. I want to stay in the background.

Fear of being seen. (I call this the "shrink back").

Low Self-Esteem
He didn't mean to hit me. I know he's sorry for what he did. He loves me.

*Fear of being alone.

Procrastination
I know I'm supposed to write a book, but I just don't have the time.

*Fear of people not listening to you or liking what you have to say. Fear of not being accepted.

Anger/Irritation
He invited me to lunch and then cancelled. I told him don't ever call me again.

*Fear of being hurt.

Can you relate to any of these statements?

The best way to overcome fear is to actually DO the thing you are afraid to do.

W.E.E.D.S. IN MY LIFE

I had a horrible fear of being seen and feared what people thought about me. Although, as a performer, i.e. acting or dancing, I did not have an issue. I could easily do these things because I was flowing in a gift and simply doing it for the love of it.

However, when it came to ministry and sharing a message or word, I was "off-script". It was "me" speaking… "me" sharing my heart… not a character or a dance I was "performing" but "me".

In my mind I would think, "Who would really want to listen to "me"?

God wanted me to begin creating videos for ministry, but I just couldn't get started. I had a secret aversion to cameras capturing "me".

I had overcome the fear of speaking in front of people thanks to Mother Omedaur Adams, who began to invite me to speak at her ministry.

However, for some reason I was paralyzed with fear at the thought of ministering on video. I think part of it had to do with the fact that it "lives on" past the moment it's created.

Also, in this age of social media, people are free to share their opinions of you and I was afraid of criticism.

As a young person, I knew I liked the arts but beyond that, I had no clue as to who I was, what I was capable of, nor my potential… and I certainly didn't know or feel that I was beautiful.

In a way, I thought "nothing" of myself. I was apathetic in a sense and truly void of identity.

As I sought the Lord about the root of this fear, certain phrases would come to mind…

"Don't think you're cute."
"She thinks she's cute."
"You ain't cute."

Hearing these kinds of words, whether spoken in seriousness or in jest, developed in me what I call the "shrink back". It caused me to want to hide in the background. I didn't want people to think that I thought I was "cute", especially when I didn't.

Side note: Within the African-American community, statements like these are often directed at girls that are "light" in complexion and have "long hair". It's still an issue in our community but there is continuing conversation around the light skinned/dark skinned issue. I believe, overall, there is an awakening and acceptance to the beauty in the spectrum of color within our ethnicity, both outside of our community, as well as inside.

The issue with hearing these types of statements was that I never had those kinds of thoughts about myself and often wondered why someone would even say something like that to me. It only served to further damaged my non-existent self-esteem. (i.e. They were bad seeds that produced W.E.E.D.S.!)

Of course, now I understand that these kinds of words are often projected at others out of the senders own issues with identity, insecurity, and/or jealousy, etc.

The feelings that no one would want to listen to me and not wanting to be seen were manifestations of those bad seeds.

Understanding why I felt this way empowered me. I was able to kill the W.E.E.D.S. with the truth of the Word of God and uproot the fear by completing a video!

Again, the word says that we perish for a lack of knowledge. It also says in all your getting, get understanding!

Knowledge and understanding are often your strongest ammunition.

Upon completing my first ministry video, the Lord gave me a dream to show me that I had indeed conquered the fear!

Honestly, after completing it, I wondered to myself, "What was I afraid of?" It felt good to operate in my calling and I began to feel more comfortable the more I did them.

As someone once said, fear is truly False Evidence Appearing Real.

W.E.E.D.S. KILLER

I want you to think about 5 W.E.E.D.S., i.e. random thoughts, excuses, or discouraging words that seem to "pop up" and could negatively affect your growth as you are trying to move forward.

1.

2.

3.

4.

5.

Next, list 5 positive seeds, or truths, that directly oppose each of the W.E.E.D.S. previously listed. Meditate on these for the next 30 days.

*Tip: Display these where you can see them everyday (maybe on your refrigerator or bathroom mirror) and say one or two aloud each time you see them.

1.

2.

3.

4.

5.

Develop a strategy against negative thoughts and negative people. Use wisdom and guard your peace and your focus!

Just as W.E.E.D.S are "determined to stifle" you, you must be more determined to break free of them!

I encourage you to seize every day and understand that with each new day, you have a fresh start, and ANYTHING is possible!

PRAYER FOR FOCUS

Father,
Thank You for renewing my mind! Help me to cast down every negative thought and vain imagination that would hinder me from moving forward; from becoming the woman You so lovingly created me to be! Help me guard my time, focus, and energy and give me the wisdom, knowledge, and understanding that I need to be more productive.

You are wonderful in all of Your ways and I give You glory for what You are doing in my life! In Jesus' name! Amen.

Chapter 7

Your Greatest Beauty

1 Corinthians 13:13 But for now, three things last — trust, hope, love; and the greatest of these is love.

According to a recent survey by the Unilever brand, Dove, only 4% of women around the world consider themselves "beautiful".

Are you a part of that 4% or are you included in the 96% that may use a different word to describe yourself?

Our definition of beauty is generally shaped by the world and the images that are most prevalent in media. These images generally promote external "ideals". Being a smart woman or a woman with character is rarely promoted as "beautiful", although I do believe there are movements today that are helping to pave the way for change in this area.

Completely unaware of how these entities influence culture and society's way of thinking, they too shaped my definition of beauty.

When I was a child, I desired blonde, straight hair and blue eyes. This was the most promoted standard of beauty I saw growing up.

It wasn't until I was a teenager watching an episode of an NAACP Image Award show (National Association for the Advancement of Colored People) that I had an epiphany about my ethnicity.

Here African-American people were beautifully acknowledging and validating one other… our gifts and accomplishments were being celebrated. I marveled at it and felt inspired.

Watching the program helped my view of myself as an African-American, but I still had a long way to go in regard to the view of myself as a woman… as Alicia.

No matter your ethnicity, you may have had similar issues growing up, which may still affect you today.

If you had curly hair, maybe you wanted straight hair… if you had brown eyes, maybe you wanted blue… if you were a size ten, perhaps you wanted to be a size two.

Whatever was being largely promoted that you did not possess, may have made you feel inadequate and even hate how you were made.

Listen, God wants you to understand the truth about beauty… not feed into the lie of what the world and the media want you to believe!

HEY BEAUTIFUL!

What is your definition of beauty? How does it line up with God's definition and what *He* says about you?

After this journey, I hope you can see just how valuable you are! You are beautiful, uniquely made, and loved by God!

His definition and standard of beauty are much different than the world's standard. In fact, when it comes to beauty, the bible says this …

1 Peter 3:3-4

3 Your beauty should not consist in externals such as fancy hairstyles, gold jewelry or what you wear; 4 rather, let it be the inner character of your heart, with the imperishable quality of a gentle and quiet spirit. In God's sight this is of great value.

Please understand this does not mean that you cannot style your hair, or wear jewelry and nice clothes. The truth is that you represent a King! You are royalty! You *should* look like a Queen!

In fact, the word also calls you an ambassador of His kingdom. You should care about how you represent God, His kingdom, and yourself!

However, this scripture is admonishing the fact that your GREATEST BEAUTY comes from within.

GENTLE AND QUIET? ME?

The scripture says that a gentle and quiet spirit is not only an imperishable quality, which means it endures forever, but it also says this quality is of great value to God!

A gentle and quiet spirit does not equate to being weak or being a pushover. It speaks of an internal state of being… how you process and handle information and circumstances.

It is one of the strongest states you can embody. When you can learn to master your emotions and respond instead of react, you can rule your world!

Proverbs 16:32
He who controls his temper is better than a war hero, he who rules his spirit better than he who captures a city.

Let's examine these qualities a little closer. Proverbs 15:1 tells us that a gentle response deflects fury, but a harsh word makes tempers rise.

Have you ever been arguing with a person, both of you yelling at the top of your lungs, and suddenly lower your voice? What happened in that situation?

Generally, the other person will either lower their voice too, or they will get so upset that you are no longer participating in the "madness" that they will leave your presence.

You have managed the situation in a way that will place you in control of you! *(Self-control is a fruit of the Spirit of God.)*

This is the power of a gentle and quiet spirit.

THE BEAUTY SECRET OF LOVE

In essence, external accoutrements should not be the driving force of your beauty, but ultimately it is the Spirit of God within you.

When the disciples asked Jesus, "What is the greatest commandment?", he replied...

Matthew 22:37-39...
He told him, "'You are to love Adonai your God with all your heart and with all your soul and with all your strength.' 38 This is the greatest and most important mitzvah. 39 And a second is similar to it, 'You are to love your neighbor as yourself.'

You may be able to say that you love God, but the real question is... do you love yourself... with all your heart, all your soul, and with all of your mind?

Let's examine **1 Corinthians 13:4-7**, also known as "The Love Chapter".

4 Love is patient and kind, not jealous, not boastful, 5 not proud, rude or selfish, not easily angered, and it keeps no record of wrongs. 6 Love does not gloat over other people's sins but takes its delight in the truth. 7 Love always bears up, always trusts, always hopes, always endures.

Questions for you to ponder:

Are you patient with yourself?
Are you kind to yourself?
Are you humble?
Do you honor yourself?
Do you get angry with yourself and condemn yourself?
Do you easily forgive yourself?
Are you a champion of the truth about yourself?
Are you hopeful about you and your future?
Does your love persevere in the face of challenges?

When you can learn to love yourself according to this scripture, it becomes easier to extend this love to others.

You know how you can tell when your friends are "in love" because they have that special glow? Well, because God is love and light, the same principle applies when you really love yourself, you shine from the inside! The more that His love fills you, the more beautiful you become.

I challenge you to practice loving yourself this way!

LOVE IS YOUR GREATEST BEAUTY!

PERMISSION TO BLOOM

Earlier, I referenced validation. Validation is the recognition or affirmation that a person or their feelings or opinions are valid or worthwhile.

Sometimes it can be difficult to move forward because you feel as though you need validation or permission from someone in authority over you.

This is natural. As a child, you probably needed permission to do anything. You needed it from your parents or guardians, your teachers, sometimes, even your peers.

When you become an adult, you need permission from your employer at some point, and even if you are an entrepreneur, you may require permission from your clients.

And yes… if you are married, sometimes you will need permission from your spouse.

Regardless, most of your life has been about requiring permission.

I am here to make an announcement…

YOU HAVE PERMISSION FROM GOD TO BE WHO HE CREATED YOU TO BE!

If you want to start a business, do it! If you want to become a writer, do it! If you want to be an inventor, do it!

Take your newfound freedom and GO, and BE, and DO whatever God has placed in your heart!

You can surely do ALL things through Christ who strengthens you! God is with you and the heavens are open for you! There is NO LIMIT to what you can achieve in GOD!

He is the DIVINE AUTHORITY and PERMISSION HAS BEEN GRANTED!

SOME MAINTENANCE REQUIRED

As we discussed, flowers need certain ingredients to flourish, and they also need pruning.

Pruning is the process of cutting away dead and overgrown stems or branches, with the ultimate purpose of increasing fruitfulness and growth.

And that, my friend, is what God wants out of our lives!

John 15:2
Every branch which is part of me but fails to bear fruit, he cuts off; and every branch that does bear fruit, he prunes, so that it may bear more fruit.

Along your journey, do not be surprised if God prunes you every now and then to be sure you are producing as much fruit as possible.

Pruning isn't comfortable. In fact, it can be painful. But always remember that God loves you, He is with you in the process, and He has the best intentions for you.

I prophesy to you that your life will be fruitful! You will have EVIDENCE of fruitfulness! Evidence of peace! Evidence of joy! Evidence of LOVE!
You will PROSPER, even as your soul prospers! I decree this over your life, in Jesus' name!

PRAYER FOR LOVE

Father, even as you are love, make me love. Transform me and help me to be more like you. Teach me and help me understand your ways of love. Help me to be more patient with myself; to be more kind and loving to myself, and in turn, help me to be the same way with others. Thank you for creating me with reverence and honor. Thank you for healing me and giving me a heart to love. I am blessed and honored that you love me so much! You call me your own. I am made in your image, fearfully and wonderfully! Thank you for fullness of joy and may it abound in me! I bless You, I thank You, and I love you! In Jesus' name! Amen.

Notes:_____
_____
_____
_____
_____
_____
_____
_____
_____
_____
_____
_____
_____
_____
_____
_____
_____
_____
_____
_____

And Then I Started Feeling Pretty

Notes:

Conclusion

In Full Bloom

Song of Solomon 2:12 Flowers appear on the earth; the season of singing has come, the cooing of doves is heard in our land.

Your relationship with God is so wonderfully magnificent! There will never be another relationship in your life that can rival it. You are in God's hand and He will cause you to Bloom.

The word "bloom" is defined as the time and season of your greatest beauty. You are "In Full Bloom" when you have learned to love yourself, learned to love others, and are fulfilling the divine purpose of God for your life.

It is truly a work of His Spirit to bring you into the knowledge of your identity and purpose.

Again, I didn't always feel like what I had to say mattered. However, now I confidently understand that there are women to whom this book will speak to, heal, and set free! This confidence comes from understanding my purpose in the Lord.

I can also confidently, unapologetically, and sincerely look in a mirror, give myself a big ole' hug, and say, "I love you, Alicia! You're beautiful!"

A dear friend pointed out to me as I was finishing this book that "Linda" (my birth mother's name) means "PRETTY" in the Spanish language.

WOW! Look at God! It made me feel as though I've truly come full circle, not only in my identity, but as a part of her legacy. Praise God!

YOUR NEXT STEPS

If God has blessed you through this book and you have received healing, breakthrough, resolve, or new revelations, let me (possibly) be one of the first to say CONGRATULATIONS! There is space for you to journal your testimony on pages 127-128.

Also, please contact me at my website and share your testimony! I would love to hear it!

www.AliciaRedmondMinistries.com

On my website, you can sign-up for my newsletter to be empowered with encouragement, inspiration, information, and of course, lots of love!

If you would like further assistance to cultivate your relationship with God and discover your gifts and purpose, be sure to stay connected!

We have an annual summer conference called **Bloom Women's Event!** We also have workshops and coaching available to help you become the woman that God has created you to be and fulfill your purpose!

I leave you with two sentiments.

First…**Ecclesiastes 3:11**
He has made everything beautiful in its own time.

I want you to notice the scripture reads "has made". This is a present tense statement. You must realize that you, my friend, are already beautiful… you were made that way. Now is your time to SEE just how beautiful you are.

And second, as you read the following poem, written in 2009 when the Father first spoke "Bloom" to me, I pray that you will receive it from the Father's heart directly to yours.

Bloom

In God's special garden
There was once a special seed
And He knew this special seed
Would serve a very special need.
So, He planted and tilled
And He pruned and watered
For you see this special seed
Was an extra special daughter!
She loved the glory of His Presence
And she basked within His light
And although the process hurt sometimes
She knew that it was right.

And on this special day
In the midst of many flowers
God proclaimed in the heavens,
"It's My special seed's hour!"

And He held her in His hand
As she reached high for her Father
He knew that she was ready
And Oh! How much He loved her!
"The time is perfect", He declared,
"No not one moment too soon…
ARISE now My lovely daughter,
It's YOUR TIME TO BLOOM!"

My Testimony

And Then I Started Feeling Pretty

About the Author

Alicia Redmond is the founder of Alicia Redmond Ministries and Bloom Women's Ministry. Upon receiving Jesus as her Savior in 1995, it was through a series of dreams that Alicia became aware of the Apostolic call on her life and in 2000, she began serving in ministry.

She has a mandate to teach others how to worship God... that is ... having relationship with God and fulfilling our purpose in Him. Her calling also extends to the areas of Arts and Entertainment and Media.

You can find her first book, Praise On Stage, The Beginner's Guide to Planning an Effective Production, on Amazon, and she is completing her upcoming book, Your Dreams Speak, A Biblical Foundation in the Study and Significance of Dreams and Dream Interpretation.

For further information or to contact Alicia, please visit her website at AliciaRedmondMinistries.com. If you would prefer to email her directly, you may do so at info@AliciaRedmondMinistries.com.

And Then I Started Feeling Pretty

Does God still speak through dreams? **YES!** If you are a "Dreamer" or would like to learn more about dreams and dream interpretation this book is for you!

Upcoming NEW Release
"Your Dreams Speak"

Visit www.AliciaRedmondMinistries.com for more information.

If you can understand your dreams, you can understand, and CHANGE, your life! — Alicia Redmond

Are you planning a stage production (dance productions included) and not sure where to start? This book will give you a basic knowledge of who and what you need, from conception to manifestation, to plan an excellent production.

"Praise On Stage"

Available at

And Then I Started Feeling Pretty

My beautiful Linda

Bloom House Books

"Books by women, for women."

If you are interested in becoming a
Bloom House Author,
please visit us at

www.AliciaRedmondMinistries.com

www.ingramcontent.com/pod-product-compliance
Lightning Source LLC
Chambersburg PA
CBHW051404290426
44108CB00015B/2146